D1469438

TOUGH DOGS

# PIT BULLS

Julie Fiedler

The Rosen Publishing Group's
**PowerKids Press**™
New York

*For Gama & Swish and Grandma & Grandpa*

Published in 2006 by The Rosen Publishing Group, Inc.
29 East 21st Street, New York, NY 10010

First Edition

Editor: Jennifer Way
Book Design: Elana Davidian

Photo Credits: Cover (left), p. 4 (top) © Ralph Reinhold/Animals Animals; Cover (right), pp. 4 (bottom),
7 (top) © J. & P. Wegner/Animals Animals; p. 7 (bottom) © Robert Pearcey/Animals Animals; p. 8 © Private
Collection, The Stapleton Collection/Bridgeman Art Library; p. 11 (top) © Corbis; p. 11 (bottom) © Swim Ink/Corbis;
pp. 12, 15 (bottom) © AP/Wide World Photos; p. 15 (top) © Henry Ausloos/Animals Animals; p. 16 © Henry Ray
Abrams/Stringer/Reuters/Corbis; p. 19 © Michael Cogliantry/Getty Images; p. 20 © Corbis Sygma.

Library of Congress Cataloging-in-Publication Data

Fiedler, Julie.
  Pit bulls / Julie Fiedler.— 1st ed.
     p. cm. — (Tough dogs)
  Includes index.
  ISBN 1-4042-3117-X (lib. bdg.)
  1.  Pit bull terriers—Juvenile literature.  I. Title.

  SF429.P58F54 2006
  636.755'9—dc22
                                    2004025435

Manufactured in the United States of America

# Contents

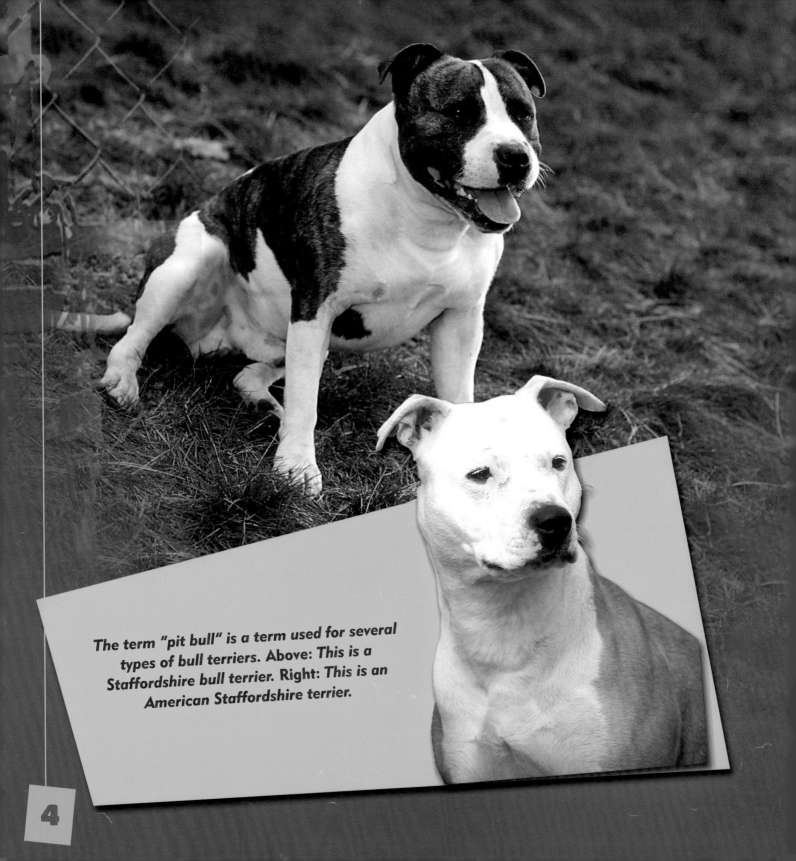

The term "pit bull" is a term used for several types of bull terriers. Above: This is a Staffordshire bull terrier. Right: This is an American Staffordshire terrier.

The pit bull is a **breed** of dog known for its bravery, intelligence, and strength. Some people believe that pit bulls are **dangerous**. That is mostly because they have heard bad stories about them in the news and do not know the breed well.

"Pit bull" is a common term for several different breeds, such as the Staffordshire bull terrier and the American pit bull terrier. Sometimes people say "pit bull" when they are talking about mixed breeds that are not related to pit bulls at all.

Pit bulls have many wonderful **qualities**. They enjoy different activities, such as working, running, and playing. Pit bulls are active, yet gentle. They are also **loyal** to their owners. A properly trained pit bull can be a joy to have as a pet and a helper. This book will show you this wonderful breed.

Pit bulls are very strong with medium-size bodies. They are usually around 18 inches (46 cm) tall and have thick bodies. In general females weigh 30 to 50 pounds (14–23 kg) and males weigh 35 to 60 pounds (16–27 kg). They are stronger than any other dogs their size. Some 60-pound (27 kg) pit bulls have been able to pull more than 2,000 pounds (907 kg)!

Both puppy and adult pit bulls have short coats that can be any color, such as white, brown, or black. They do not have special markings, but they can have spots or be a solid color. Their tails are cut, or docked, when they are young. They have thick, flat heads, broad shoulders, and wide jaws. From the front their faces look heart-shaped or triangular. Their ears are naturally floppy. Owners often crop pit bull puppies' ears to give them a pointed look. They have almond-shaped eyes that can be any color except blue.

Pit bulls can be many colors and can have many different markings. Left: These are Staffordshire terrier puppies. Above: This American Staffordshire terrier is a strongly built adult.

7

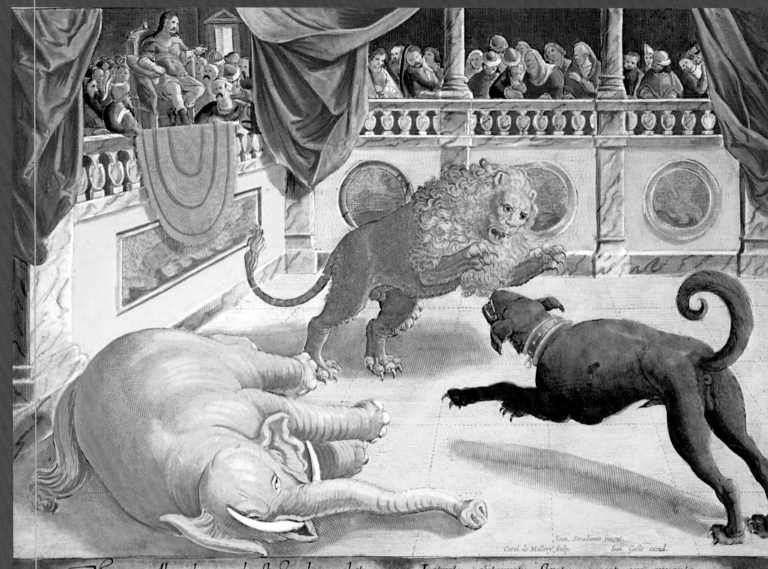

Magnus Alexander populo spectacula præbet.
Concertant. Canis et Barrus : Barrum Canis acer
Latratu exterret, stratum necat ore cruento.
Quin etiam rabidum superat... ...onem.

The Romans used dogs that are believed to be the ancestors of the pit bull in a sport called baiting. This painting from the 1500s shows one of these tough dogs battling a lion.

# Ancestors of the Pit Bull

During ancient times dogs were very different from the ones we see today. Some of these ancient dogs became the **ancestors** of today's breeds. The pit bull's ancestors were fighting dogs.

In Greece during the third century B.C., there were large dogs called Mollossians. These dogs were guard dogs that fought in battles. They were brought to other parts of the world, such as Britain. When the Romans attacked Britain around A.D. 43, they brought some of these dogs back to Italy. These dogs fought against bulls, bears, and lions in a sport called baiting. These ancient dogs are believed to be the ancestors of some of today's toughest dogs. Their strength and appearance resembled those of the pit bull, the bulldog, and the mastiff.

*Dogs were domesticated from wolves about 15,000 years ago. All modern dog breeds are descended from the wolf.*

9

# History of the Pit Bull

*Dog fighting is now against the law in the United States and in many other places. Such laws help keep dogs from mistreatment by people. Fighting is dangerous for the dogs, who can be hurt or even killed in a fight.*

Pit bulls as we know them today started to appear in the early 1800s in Britain. People wanted fighting dogs that would be as **aggressive** as bulldogs and as active as terriers. They bred bulldogs and terriers to make pit bulls, which have both qualities.

Pit bulls were used for many activities other than fighting, such as hunting and herding. They are very gentle toward people but can be aggressive toward other animals. They helped farmers guard their land from other animals, such as wolves.

When pit bulls were brought to the United States from Europe in the mid 1800s, they helped American settlers on their farms. During **World War I** and **World War II** pit bulls worked with soldiers. During that time, there were many cartoons that featured pit bull characters.

English Bulldog

German Dachshund

American Bull Terrier

French Bulldog

Russian Wolf-Hound

I'm Neutral, BUT-Not Afraid of any of them.

WALLACE ROBINSON-1915

**Above: General Patton brought his bull terrier, Willie, with him in World War II. Left: In this poster dogs stand for the countries fighting in World War I. The Harrison bull terrier in the center stands for the United States.**

11

This pit bull, right, is part of a group of dogs used to provide pet therapy to children. Pit bulls are often chosen for this job because their intelligence makes them easy to train. They are also gentle and friendly.

# Pit Bulls Today

Pit bulls are still one of the most popular breeds in the United States. They make wonderful pets and working dogs. Some pit bulls help farmers look after livestock, just as they did during pioneer days. They have also become popular pets across the United States. Certain groups have events for dogs that measure different abilities, such as **agility**, **obedience**, and strength. Many pit bulls have won these events.

Because pit bulls are friendly and open to training, they are very good at **pet therapy**. They visit hospitals and nursing homes to cheer up patients. They also are hearing dogs for the deaf. Pit bulls are also very useful to police and rescue workers and make excellent rescue dogs. Pit bulls help people in many different ways. Because there have been harmful news stories about pit bulls, some people have become afraid of the breed, in spite of their good work.

13

# A Misunderstood Breed

The qualities of loyalty and bravery that make pit bulls such wonderful pets and workers have been used against them. Careless owners have made people think of pit bulls as naturally aggressive dogs. Because pit bulls are such powerful dogs, some owners teach them to attack. The use of dogs for fighting has been illegal for more than 100 years. Owners should not train dogs to fight. Some owners mistreat pit bulls, which can make them aggressive toward people. Many different kinds of dogs have bitten people, but the news most often reports stories with pit bulls. This is because they are so powerful and can cause a lot of harm. Therefore, some people believe that this breed is mean by nature.

The truth is that pit bulls are loving, gentle, and obedient dogs that can be easily trained. They can be very loyal to their owners. It is up to the owners to take good care of their pit bulls and to raise them carefully.

**Above:** *Pit bull puppies need to be trained at a young age.* **Right:** *This pit bull was mistreated by his owners and trained to fight and act aggressively.*

Pit bulls need lots of exercise to stay healthy and happy. They can be a good pet for people who enjoy jogging and who like to bring their dogs with them on their runs.

# Caring for a Pit Bull

It is important to care for dogs properly, no matter which breed they are. Good care requires providing shelter, healthy food, water, love, and obedience training to prevent bad behavior. Pit bulls should be brushed at least once a week and bathed every one to two months. Owners must also make sure their dogs visit the **veterinarian** for regular checkups.

Pit bulls are great for active people because they have lots of energy. Owners should provide one to three hours of exercise every day by walking, running, and playing with their pit bulls. Exercise keeps pit bulls strong and happy. If pit bulls do not get enough exercise, they might behave badly.

## DOG SAFETY TIPS

- Never approach a dog you do not know.
- When meeting a dog for the first time, offer your hand for the dog to smell.
- Speak softly, not loudly. Move gently, not suddenly.
- Never try to pet a dog through a fence.
- Never bother a dog while it is sleeping, eating, or sick.
- Do not pull at a dog's fur, ears, or tail. Never tease or hit a dog.
- Never approach a dog that is growling or showing its teeth. Back away slowly. Yelling and running can cause the dog to chase you or act aggressively.

Pit bulls must be trained earlier in life than other breeds before they get too strong. Dog care specialists say owners should start training pit bulls when they are just a few weeks old, instead of a few months old. Owners must be aware of and in control of what their dogs are doing at all times. If owners want help, they can take their dogs to obedience school.

Another important part of raising healthy pit bulls is **socialization**. Socialization includes presenting young dogs to different people, places, and other dogs with careful guidance. Adult pit bulls are more likely to be good around new people and dogs if they are properly brought into contact with them when young. Pit bulls that are not properly socialized might act aggressively out of fear and harm someone.

Pit bulls need to be taught basic commands, such as sit, stay, and lie down. They can also learn tricks, which can be used when playing and exercising. This man is teaching his pit bull to jump.

19

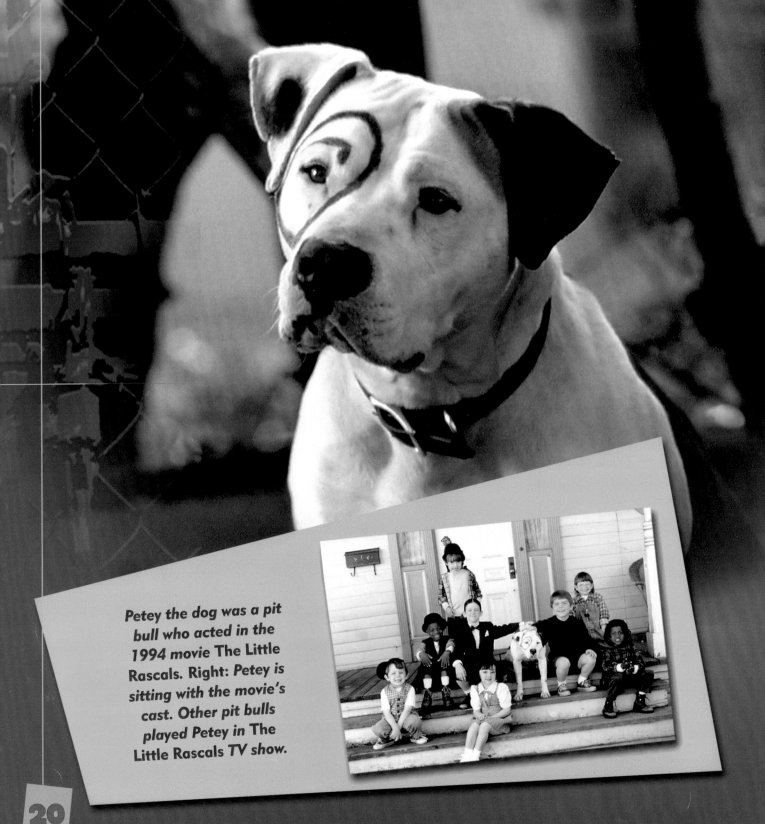

Petey the dog was a pit bull who acted in the 1994 movie The Little Rascals. Right: Petey is sitting with the movie's cast. Other pit bulls played Petey in The Little Rascals TV show.

# Famous Pit Bulls

There have been many famous pit bulls in history. A pit bull named Stubby was a hero in World War I. He was awarded prizes for his bravery and was given the rank of sergeant in the army because of his accomplishments.

A female pit bull named Weela helped save 30 people and more than 40 animals during a flood in California. Weela was a household pet. Her owners noticed she had a special ability to sense danger when no one else did. Weela guided people to safety and carried food to **stranded** animals. Her bravery helped save many lives.

Pit bulls are also very talented and make great actors. The charming dog from the old TV show called *The Little Rascals*, Petey, was a pit bull.

*Many famous people have owned pit bulls, including writer Laura Ingalls Wilder, writer Helen Keller, inventor Thomas Edison, President Theodore Roosevelt, actor Michael J. Fox, and actor Frankie Muniz from Malcolm in the Middle.*

Pit bulls have captured the hearts of many people throughout the world. They make wonderful family dogs and also perform great public services.

A pit bull named Starfire is a great example of this outstanding breed. In the 1990s, she won two events called the Grand Championship and the National Championship. Every year she attended a pet fair. She showed people what a friendly dog she was and helped teach people about pit bulls. Starfire also made visits to a children's home to lift the spirits of the children. Starfire was quite a dog!

There are about 750 pit bulls listed with the American Kennel Club. Many of them are working dogs. Pit bulls are tough, but people should value and respect them. Now that you know more about pit bulls, you can help teach others about this breed.

# Glossary

**aggressive** (uh-GREH-siv)  Ready to fight.

**agility** (uh-JIH-lih-tee)  The property of being able to move around quickly and easily.

**ancestors** (AN-ses-terz)  Relatives who lived long ago.

**breed** (BREED)  A group of animals that look alike and have the same relatives.

**dangerous** (DAYN-jer-us)  Able to cause harm.

**loyal** (LOY-ul)  Faithful to a person or an idea.

**obedience** (oh-BEE-dee-ents)  Willingness to do what you are told to do.

**pet therapy** (PET THER-uh-pee)  When people use animals to help them deal with certain problems.

**qualities** (KWAH-luh-teez)  Features that make something or someone special.

**socialization** (soh-shuh-lih-ZAY-shun)  Learning to be friendly.

**stranded** (STRAN-ded)  Left alone in a scary or hard state.

**veterinarian** (veh-tuh-ruh-NER-ee-un)  A doctor who treats animals.

**World War I** (WURLD WOR WUN)  The war fought in Europe from 1914 to 1918.

**World War II** (WURLD WOR TOO)  A war fought by the United States, Great Britain, France, and the Soviet Union against Germany, Japan, and Italy from 1939 to 1945.

# Index

# Web Sites

Due to the changing nature of Internet links, PowerKids Press has developed an online list of Web sites related to the subject of this book. This site is updated regularly. Please use this link to access the list: www.powerkidslinks.com/tdog/pitbulls/